About The Author

Growing up in northern Wisconsin, I never believed I'd be advising people on how to make wise financial decisions. During my tenure in the United States Army, I found fulfillment in coaching, mentoring, and leading.

After my service ended, I was jobless for 8 months and a month away from homelessness. At this moment, I really needed to change my money habits and learn to be frugal. As you will discover, achieving success requires a great deal of discipline.

I am going to share with you my tips on what you can do to work your way to Financial Freedom Now.

Work and Education

United States Army - Infantry

Hawaiian Airlines
- Sr. Operations Managers
- Sr. Project Manager - Finance

Shidler College of Business -
Master of Business Administration (MBA)
Lean Six Sigma - Black Belt

This book is for educational purposes only

Table of Contents

The Why

Being financially savvy is a terrific place to start since it lays the groundwork for a more stable and secure future. Individuals who are financially prudent may make informed decisions regarding their money, which can lead to long-term financial success.

Understanding how to budget, save, and invest money intelligently, as well as manage debts and live within one's means, are all examples of financial intelligence. It also entails being aware of various financial products and services, as well as learning how to make informed decisions that match with personal financial objectives.

Individuals who have a firm foundation in financial literacy are more positioned to make wise financial decisions, avoid costly mistakes, and confidently plan for the future. Overall, financial responsibility is an important part of personal responsibility that can have a substantial impact on one's quality of life.

Introduction to Personal Finance

Personal Finance refers to the management of an individual's or a household's financial resources, including their income, expenses, investments, and debts. It involves making informed decisions about how to allocate and manage one's financial resources to achieve financial goals and maintain financial stability.

Personal Financial Planning is important for several reasons. First, it helps individuals to set financial goals and create a roadmap to achieve them. Second, it enables individuals to make informed decisions about spending, saving, and investing. Third, it helps individuals to avoid debt and manage existing debt more effectively. Fourth, it provides a sense of security and peace of mind, knowing that one's financial future is being actively planned and managed.

Some basic financial concepts include:

Budgeting: This involves creating a plan for how to allocate one's income and expenses, with the goal of living within one's means and achieving financial goals.

Saving: This involves setting aside a portion of one's income for future use, such as an emergency fund, retirement savings, down payment on a real estate.

Investing: This involves using one's money to purchase assets, such as stocks, bonds, or real estate, with the goal of generating a return on investment (ROI).

Debt: This refers to money that is owed to a lender or creditor, such as credit card debt or a mortgage. There is a difference between "Good Debt" and "Bad Debt" that I will make you aware of later.

Interest: This is the cost of borrowing money, or the return on investment for lending money.
 - The better your credit score, the better your interest rate.

Inflation: This refers to the rate at which the general level of prices for goods and services is rising, which can affect the value of money over time.

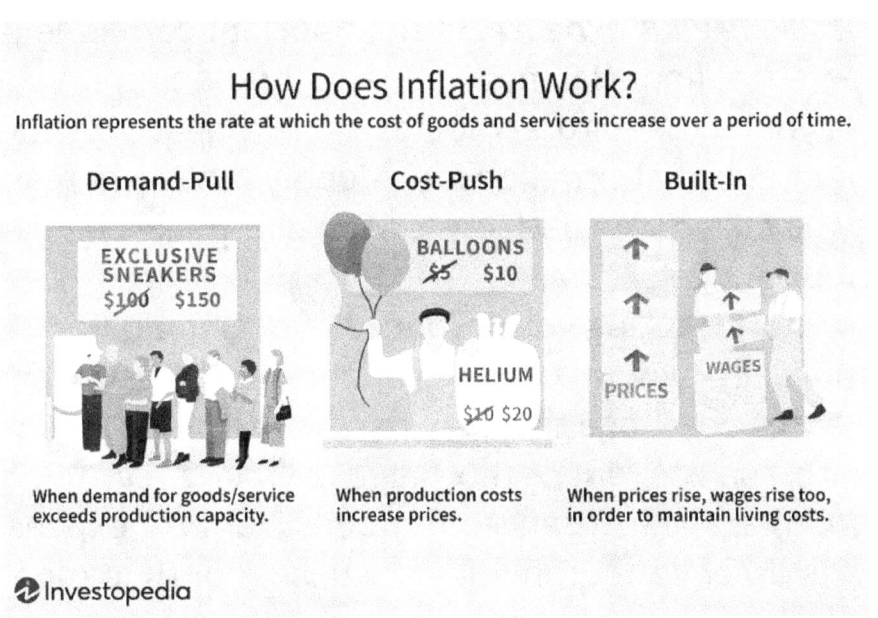

How Does Inflation Work?

Inflation represents the rate at which the cost of goods and services increase over a period of time.

Demand-Pull	Cost-Push	Built-In
EXCLUSIVE SNEAKERS $100 $150	BALLOONS $5 $10 HELIUM $10 $20	PRICES WAGES
When demand for goods/service exceeds production capacity.	When production costs increase prices.	When prices rise, wages rise too, in order to maintain living costs.

Investopedia

Budgeting

Budgeting entails developing a strategy for allocating your income and costs, with the aim of ensuring that your spending does not exceed your income. To build a budget, you must determine your fixed and variable spending, as well as your sources of revenue.

Fixed expenses, such as rent or mortgage payments, are consistent from month to month, but variable expenses, such as food and entertainment, fluctuate from month to month. Once you have determined your income and expenses, you may establish a budget using a spreadsheet, a budgeting app, or pen and paper.

- You can find excel spreadsheets on the internet that are user friendly and already build out for you!

Tracking your expenses is an important component of personal financial management. By keeping a record of all your expenditures, you can gain a clearer picture of your financial situation and identify areas where you may be able to cut back on spending or make changes to your budget.

To start tracking your expenses, you should first identify all of your fixed and variable expenses. Fixed expenses are those that stay the same from month to month, such as rent or mortgage payments, car payments, and insurance premiums. Variable expenses, on the other hand, can fluctuate from month to month and include things like groceries, entertainment, and travel expenses.

Once you have a list of all your expenses, you can start tracking them by recording every purchase or payment you make. You can use a spreadsheet, budgeting app, or a notebook to record each transaction.

It's important to be as detailed as possible, including the date, the amount spent, and what the purchase was for. Some budgeting apps can even automatically categorize your expenses, making it easier to see where your money is going.

By tracking your expenses, you can see where you may be overspending and make changes to your budget accordingly. You may find that you're spending more on dining out than you realized, for example, or that you're spending more on subscriptions than you need to. With this information, you can make adjustments to your spending habits and work towards achieving your financial goals.

An essential part of personal financial management is emergency savings. A reserve for unforeseen expenses, such as a medical emergency, car repair, or job loss. By establishing an emergency fund, you can avoid using credit cards or other kinds of debt to meet these bills, so saving money over time.

To begin saving for emergencies, you should aim to amass a fund sufficient to cover three to six months of living expenses. This may appear frightening, but you can start small and expand your savings steadily over time.

Creating a separate savings account for emergencies is one approach to begin preparing for unexpected events. This allows you to keep your emergency money distinct from your regular savings, making them easier to track and manage. You can also automate monthly transfers from your checking account to your emergency fund to make consistent saving easier.

The ultimate key to establishing an emergency fund is making it a priority and being consistent with your savings efforts. By maintaining a substantial emergency fund, you can rest assured that you're prepared for unforeseen expenses and can weather any financial storms that may arise.

Debt management is the practice of actively managing and repaying debt in a sustainable manner that allows you to reach your financial objectives. Effective debt management is creating a strategy to pay off your obligations, determining which bills to pay off first, and identifying strategies to minimize your interest rates or monthly payments.

To begin debt management, you must first compile a list of all your debts, including the total amount owing, interest rates, and minimum monthly payments. This list can be used to establish a debt repayment plan, which includes choosing which debts to pay off first.

The debt snowball approach is a popular debt repayment strategy that involves paying off the smaller obligations first and then using the money saved to pay off larger debts. The debt avalanche technique entails paying off debts with the highest interest rates first in order to save money on interest payments.

In addition to these measures, you can manage your debt by negotiating with your creditors for lower interest rates or monthly payments, consolidating your debt into a single loan with a reduced interest rate, or obtaining the advice of a credit counseling agency or debt management program.

It is important to remember that debt management requires time and work, and it is crucial to adhere to your repayment schedule. By making consistent payments, finding strategies to lower your interest rates or monthly payments, and remaining disciplined with your expenditures, you can eventually eliminate your debts and attain financial independence.

Below are three nonprofit credit counseling agencies that offer debt management plans in all 50 states:
- *American Consumer Credit Counseling*
- *Consumer Credit Counseling Service (CCCS)*
- *Navicore Solutions*

Banking and Credit

Choosing a bank is an important decision that can have a significant impact on your personal financial management. When selecting a bank, you should consider a variety of factors, such as fees, interest rates, account options, and customer service.

Here are some key factors to consider when choosing a bank:

1) Fees: Different banks charge different fees for their services, such as monthly account maintenance fees, ATM fees, and overdraft fees. Be sure to compare the fee structures of different banks to find one that offers low or no fees that fit your needs.

2) Interest rates: Banks offer different interest rates on savings and checking accounts. Consider the interest rates offered by different banks and choose one that offers competitive rates that can help you grow your savings.

3) Account options: Banks offer different types of accounts, such as checking, savings, and money market accounts. Consider the account options available at different banks to find one that fits your needs.

4) Mobile and online banking: Many banks offer mobile and online banking options, such as mobile apps, online account access, and mobile check deposit. Consider the digital banking options available at different banks to find one that offers the features you need.

5) Mobile and online banking: Many banks offer mobile and online banking options, such as mobile apps, online account access, and mobile check deposit. Consider the digital banking options available at different banks to find one that offers the features you need.

6) Customer service: Consider the quality of customer service offered by different banks, such as the availability of customer support, ease of contacting customer service, and overall customer satisfaction.

7) FDIC insurance: Make sure that the bank you choose is insured by the Federal Deposit Insurance Corporation (FDIC). This ensures that your deposits are protected up $250K in the event that the bank fails.

By considering these factors, you can choose a bank that meets your financial needs and helps you achieve your financial goals.

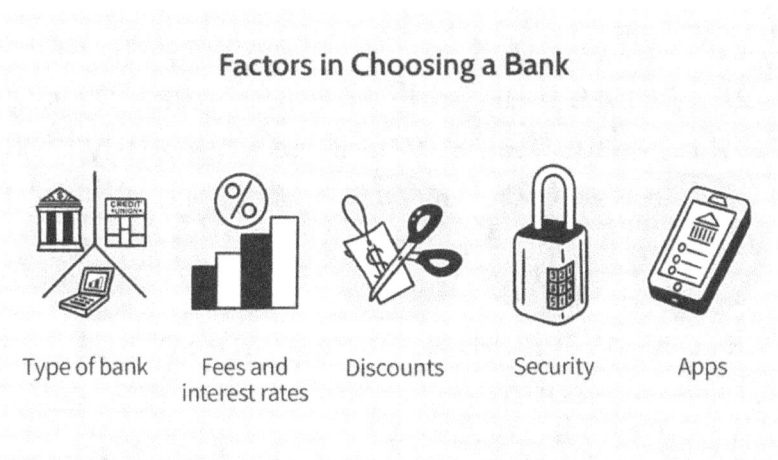

Factors in Choosing a Bank

| Type of bank | Fees and interest rates | Discounts | Security | Apps |

Investopedia

Checking and savings accounts are two common types of bank accounts that serve different purposes. Here are some key differences between the two:

Purpose: A checking account is designed for everyday transactions, such as paying bills, making purchases, and withdrawing cash. A *savings account*, on the other hand, is meant to help you save money for the future and earn interest on your savings. Regular savings accounts are NOT the way to go, on average, they typically earn about .02 to .03 percent APY.

My personal favorite is a *high-yield savings account*. It is a form of federally insured savings product that earns much higher interest rates than the national average. They can earn approximately 3% APY. In comparison, the national average savings rate is 0.33 percent APY.

If your funds are in a high-yielding account, your balance will rise without any additional work on your behalf. With a 3% APY, a $10,000 savings amount would earn slightly more than $300 after one year. It may not make you rich, but the returns are significantly higher than a 0.30 percent APY account, which would yield roughly $30.

Consequently, regular accounts earn so little interest that high-yield accounts earn 13 to 17 times more than conventional accounts.

Fees: Checking accounts may come with fees such as monthly maintenance fees, overdraft fees, and ATM fees. Savings accounts usually have fewer fees associated with them, but some banks may charge you if you exceed the monthly withdrawal limit or if your balance falls below a certain amount.

Accessibility: Checking accounts offer more convenient access to your money, such as through debit cards, online banking, and mobile apps. Savings accounts, on the other hand, may have restrictions on the number of withdrawals you can make per month and may not offer debit cards.

In general, a checking account is a good option if you need easy access to your money and plan to make frequent transactions, while a high-yield savings account is a good choice if you want to earn interest on your savings and have a long-term savings goal in mind. It's also possible to have multiple types of accounts to meet different financial needs.

My recommendation is to have a checking account at a local bank, then link it to a high-yield saving accont and it doesnt have to be at the same bank. Most online banks give you easy access to your high-yield savings account, so you can transfer money easy from bank to bank.

Credit cards and credit scores are related in that credit card usage and payment behavior can impact a person's credit score.

A credit score is a numerical value assigned to an individual that represents their creditworthiness. Credit scores are typically calculated based on a variety of factors, including payment history, credit utilization, length of credit history, types of credit used, and new credit applications. The higher the credit score, the more likely a person is to be approved for credit and receive favorable interest rates for loans.

Credit card usage can impact credit scores in several ways. One important factor is credit utilization, which is the percentage of a person's available credit that they are currently using. If someone has a high credit utilization rate, meaning they are using a lot of their available credit, it can lower their credit score. This is because high credit utilization can be an indicator that a person may be overextended and have difficulty repaying their debts.

Another factor is payment history. Late payments or missed payments on credit cards can also lower a person's credit score. On the other hand, making payments on time and in full can help improve a person's credit score over time.

In summary, credit cards can impact credit scores by affecting credit utilization and payment history. It's important for individuals to use credit cards responsibly and make payments on time in order to maintain or improve their credit scores.

Loans and mortgages are both forms of borrowing money, but there are some key differences between them.

A loan is a type of financial agreement between a borrower and a lender. The borrower receives a specific amount of money, which they agree to pay back over a set period of time, usually with interest. Loans can be secured or unsecured, meaning they may or may not require collateral to be put up as security for the loan.

Mortgages, on the other hand, are a specific type of loan that is used to finance the purchase of a property, such as a house or a condo. Mortgages are usually long-term loans with repayment periods that can span 15, 20, or 30 years, and they are typically secured by the property being purchased. This means that if the borrower fails to make their mortgage payments, the lender can seize the property to recover their money.

One key difference between loans and mortgages is the purpose of the borrowing. Loans can be used for a variety of purposes, such as paying for a car, financing a wedding, or consolidating debt. Mortgages, on the other hand, are specifically designed to finance the purchase of real estate.

Another difference is the interest rate. Mortgages typically have lower interest rates than other types of loans, because they are secured by the property being purchased, which provides collateral for the lender. This means that the lender is taking on less risk, so they can offer lower interest rates to borrowers.

While both loans and mortgages are forms of borrowing money, loans can be used for a variety of purposes, while mortgages are specifically used to finance the purchase of a property. Mortgages also typically have lower interest rates due to the collateralization of the property being purchased.

Compare your loan term options

Shorter term	Longer term
↑ Higher monthly payments	↓ Lower monthly payments
↓ Typically lower interest rates	↑ Typically higher interest rates
↓ Lower total cost	↑ Higher total cost

Investing

Stocks, bonds, and mutual funds are all different types of investments that people can use to grow their money over time. Here's a brief overview of each:

Stocks: A stock is a type of investment that represents ownership in a company. When you buy a stock, you become a shareholder in the company and have a claim on a portion of its assets and earnings. The value of a stock can rise or fall depending on the company's financial performance, the overall economy, and other factors. Stocks can be a higher-risk, higher-reward investment, and are typically best suited for long-term investors who are willing to ride out market fluctuations.

There are many platforms you can use to invest in the stock market. You can invest as little as $1 to however much you can afford. I recommend you look for stocks that pay dividends and diversifying across many industries.

Bonds: A bond is a type of investment that represents a loan made to a company or government. When you buy a bond, you are essentially lending money to the issuer, who agrees to pay you interest on the loan until the bond reaches maturity, at which point you receive the principal back. Bonds are generally considered a lower-risk investment than stocks, but also typically offer lower potential returns.

Mutual funds: A mutual fund is a type of investment vehicle that pools money from many investors to purchase a diversified portfolio of stocks, bonds, or other securities. By investing in a mutual fund, you can spread your money across a range of different investments, which can help to minimize risk. Mutual funds are managed by professional investment managers, who make decisions about which securities to buy and sell on behalf of the fund's investors.

In short, stocks, bonds, and mutual funds are all different types of investments that people can use to build wealth over time. Stocks represent ownership in a company, bonds represent loans made to a company or government, and mutual funds allow investors to pool their money to purchase a diversified portfolio of investments. Each type of investment has its own unique characteristics and risk-reward profile, so it's important to choose the one that best fits your financial goals and risk tolerance.

Typically, if you are younger, you should take on more risk when investing. The closer you are to retirement, you might not want to take as much risk considering it might take the economy longer to course correct.

Retirement planning is the process of preparing for your financial needs in your later years, when you are no longer working. Proper retirement planning can help you ensure that you have enough income to maintain your standard of living during retirement, cover medical expenses, and enjoy leisure activities.

Steps you can take to plan for retirement:

Set a retirement goal: Determine the amount of money you will need to save for retirement based on your expected expenses, anticipated lifespan, and desired lifestyle. This goal will help you to stay on track and make progress towards your retirement savings goals.

Create a retirement savings plan: Decide how much you need to save each month to reach your retirement goal. You can use tools like retirement calculators to help you estimate how much you should be saving each month to reach your retirement goal.

Start saving as soon as possible: The earlier you start saving for retirement, the more time your money has to grow. It's never too early or too late to start saving, so begin as soon as possible and save consistently.

Maximize your retirement accounts: Take advantage of employer-sponsored retirement accounts such as 401(k) plans, as well as individual retirement accounts (IRAs). These accounts offer tax-advantages and can help your money grow faster.

Consider diversifying your investments: Diversification helps to spread out risk, and can help you avoid investing all your savings in a single asset class. You can invest in a mix of stocks, bonds, and other asset classes based on your risk tolerance and financial goals.

Regularly review and adjust your plan: Make sure to regularly review and adjust your retirement plan based on your changing circumstances, such as changes in your expenses, income, or investment performance.

Retirement planning is the process of preparing for your financial needs in your later years. By setting retirement goals, creating a savings plan, maximizing retirement accounts, diversifying your investments, and regularly reviewing and adjusting your plan, you can ensure that you have a comfortable retirement.

A good rule of thumb is to save 15% of your annual gross income. In an ideal world, saving would begin in one's twenties and continue throughout one's working years.

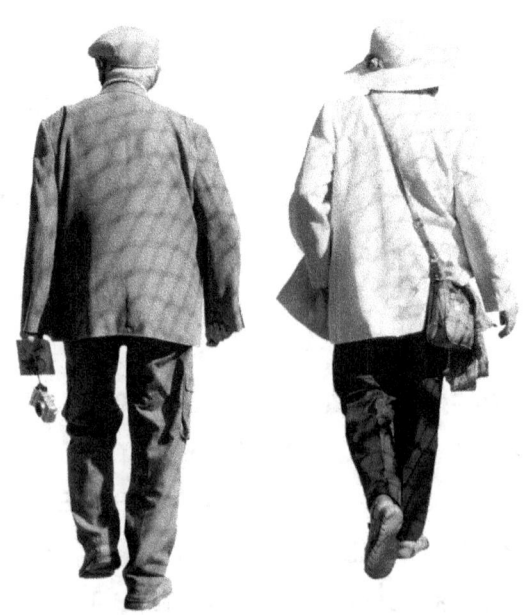

Tax-advantaged accounts are specialized investment accounts that offer tax benefits to investors. Here are some of the most common types of tax-advantaged accounts:

401(k) Plans: These are employer-sponsored retirement plans that allow you to contribute a portion of your salary on a pre-tax basis. This reduces your taxable income, and the money in the account grows tax-free until it's withdrawn.

Traditional IRAs: These are individual retirement accounts that allow you to contribute pre-tax money, which reduces your taxable income. The money grows tax-free until it's withdrawn during retirement, at which point it is taxed as ordinary income.

Roth IRAs: These are also individual retirement accounts, but contributions are made with after-tax money. The money in the account grows tax-free, and qualified withdrawals in retirement are also tax-free.

Health Savings Accounts (HSAs): These are savings accounts that can be used to pay for qualifying medical expenses. Contributions to an HSA are tax-deductible, and the money grows tax-free. Withdrawals for qualifying medical expenses are also tax-free.

529 Plans: These are education savings plans that offer tax benefits for saving for education expenses. Contributions to a 529 plan grow tax-free, and withdrawals for qualified education expenses are also tax-free. Families can make a tax-free rollover from 529 plans to Roth individual retirement accounts starting in 2024, maximum of $35K.

By taking advantage of these types of tax-advantaged accounts, you can reduce your tax bill, save money on taxes over time, and better prepare for future expenses like retirement or education. It's important to understand the specific rules and regulations of each type of tax-advantaged account, as well as any contribution limits or eligibility requirements.

Investing can be a great way to build wealth over time, but it's important to approach it with a thoughtful and informed strategy. Here are some tips to help you build wealth through investing:

Start early: The earlier you start investing, the more time your money has to grow. This is due to the power of compounding, which allows your investments to earn interest on top of interest over time.

Diversify your portfolio: Diversification is key to managing risk and maximizing returns. By investing in a variety of different assets, such as stocks, bonds, and real estate, you can reduce your exposure to any one particular risk and increase your overall returns.

Invest in what you know: It's important to understand the investments you're making. If you don't have a good grasp of a particular industry or asset class, you may be taking on more risk than you realize. Do your own market research on to get a better understanding.

Keep costs low: Fees and commissions can eat into your investment returns over time. Look for low-cost investment options, such as index funds or ETFs, and avoid high-fee investments like actively managed mutual funds. There are also a number of apps and investment firms that waive fees or dont have any fees to invest.

Stay the course: Investing is a long-term game, and it's important to stay committed to your investment strategy even when markets are volatile. Trying to time the market or chase hot stocks is often a losing strategy in the long run.

There are many different strategies depenting on the amount of risk you want to assume. I choose to invest in companies for a 5 to 10 year deration, then consistently study the market for the next investment.

Seek professional advice: If you're not comfortable managing your investments on your own, consider working with a financial advisor or investment professional who can help you create a tailored investment plan that aligns with your goals and risk tolerance.

Financial advisors or planners advise individuals on wealth management and other personal financial matters. Financial advisors/advisers are able to draft strategies and offer specific investment products and vehicles to match their clients needs.

Some charge a flat fee whenever they complete a transaction or sell you a goods. Others charge an hourly fee or a fee based on the amount of money they manage.

While a sound financial plan can be an investment, some financial advisors drive increase expenses by suggesting frequent asset turnover or directing clients toward more costly (high-fee) options.

If you pick a financial adviser, you must always ensure that he or she complies with fiduciary standards and legal requirements to operate in your best interests and discloses any potential conflicts of interest. Importantly, financial advisors are only held to the criterion of suitability.

Insurance

Insurance is an important tool for managing risk and protecting yourself and your assets in case of unexpected events. Here's a brief overview of some common types of insurance:

Health Insurance: Health insurance helps cover the cost of medical care, including doctor visits, hospitalizations, and prescription drugs. This can be especially important if you or a family member experiences a serious illness or injury that requires expensive medical treatments. Depending on the plan, health insurance may be purchased through your employer, a private insurer, or the government.

Life Insurance: Life insurance provides financial support for your loved ones if you pass away. The policy pays out a lump sum to your beneficiaries, who can use the money to cover expenses like funeral costs, outstanding debts, or ongoing living expenses. There are two main types of life insurance: term life insurance, which provides coverage for a specific period of time, and permanent life insurance, which provides coverage for your entire life.

Disability Insurance: Disability insurance provides income replacement if you are unable to work due to a disability. This can help cover expenses like rent or mortgage payments, utilities, and groceries while you are unable to earn a regular income. Depending on the policy, disability insurance may be short-term or long-term.

Financial Planning for Major Life Events

Planning for College: College can be expensive, but there are several ways to prepare financially. Consider starting a college savings account, such as a 529 plan, as early as possible to give your savings time to grow. You may also want to research scholarships, grants, and student loans to help cover the costs of tuition, fees, and other expenses.

Getting Married: Getting married can impact your finances in several ways, from joint tax returns to shared expenses. Make sure to have open and honest conversations with your partner about your financial goals and expectations, including how you plan to manage your money together. You may also want to consider creating a prenuptial agreement to protect your assets and clarify financial responsibilities.

Starting a Family: Having a child can be a wonderful and rewarding experience, but it also comes with new financial challenges. Consider budgeting for expenses like child care, medical bills, and education. You may also want to look into life insurance, disability insurance, and estate planning to ensure your family is protected in case of unexpected events.

Planning for Retirement: Retirement planning is important for everyone, regardless of age. Start by estimating how much you'll need to save for retirement based on your expected expenses and lifestyle. Consider contributing to a tax-advantaged retirement account, such as a 401(k) or IRA. You may also want to work with a financial advisor who can help you create a personalized retirement plan based on your goals and risk tolerance.

Putting It All Together

Creating a personal financial plan can help you achieve your financial goals and build long-term wealth. Here are some steps to develop, implement, and adjust your financial plan:

Developing a Personal Financial Plan: Start by setting clear financial goals and identifying the steps you need to take to achieve them. This may include creating a budget, paying off debt, saving for retirement or a down payment on a home, or investing in the stock market. Consider working with a financial advisor or using online tools to help you create a personalized financial plan that aligns with your goals and risk tolerance.

Implementing Financial Strategies: Once you have a financial plan in place, it's important to take action to make it a reality. This may include setting up automatic savings contributions, creating a debt repayment plan, or choosing investment accounts that align with your goals and risk tolerance. Be sure to track your progress and adjust your plan as needed to stay on track.

Reassessing and Adjusting Your Plan: Life is unpredictable, and your financial plan may need to change as your circumstances change. Be sure to review your plan regularly and adjust it as needed based on changes in your income, expenses, or goals. This may include adjusting your budget, reallocating investments, or updating your estate planning documents.

By developing, implementing, and adjusting your personal financial plan, you can build long-term wealth and achieve your financial goals. Remember to stay focused on your goals, stay disciplined with your financial strategy, and seek guidance from a financial professional if you need it. Do your due diligence, thank you for reading!

Notes:

Notes: